IMAGES
of America

KINGFISHER AND KINGFISHER COUNTY

Simon Peter Leitner came to the area with the land run of 1889, at first getting a lot in the town of Kingfisher and later settling on a homestead to the west of town with his son-in-law Josiah "Barefoot" Williams. Here he is shown with his grandchildren. From left to right are (first row) Josiah Williams, Andrew Williams, and Neoma Williams; (second row) Simon Williams, Leitner, and Lynore Williams. For more information on how rough Leitner had things at first, see page 30. (Courtesy Chisholm Trail Museum, Kingfisher.)

On the cover: Finished in 1903, this was the third courthouse of Kingfisher County, and it existed until 1959. In front is A. E. Stalnaker, the man who surveyed the courthouse. (Courtesy Chisholm Trail Museum, Kingfisher.)

IMAGES
of America

KINGFISHER AND KINGFISHER COUNTY

Glen V. McIntyre

ARCADIA
PUBLISHING

Copyright © 2009 by Glen V. McIntyre
ISBN 978-1-5316-3950-1

Published by Arcadia Publishing
Charleston, South Carolina

Library of Congress Catalog Card Number: 2008934223

For all general information contact Arcadia Publishing at:
Telephone 843-853-2070
Fax 843-853-0044
E-mail sales@arcadiapublishing.com
For customer service and orders:
Toll-Free 1-888-313-2665

Visit us on the Internet at www.arcadiapublishing.com

To Mom and Dad

CONTENTS

ACKNOWLEDGMENTS

First I want to acknowledge Ginger Murphy and Renee Mitchell for their help at the Chisholm Trail Museum going through its extensive photograph collection, and I want to thank them for permission to use the photographs in this book. Murphy has also loaned the image of the Simon Peter Leitner homestead, which provides such graphic evidence of how hard things were at first.

I also want to thank Jeremy Ingle of the *Kingfisher Times and Free Press*, who serves as president of the Chisholm Trail Museum, for donating all of one Saturday to scanning a large group of these photographs and helping to answer questions about Dover.

I want to acknowledge William Welge, director of archives at the Oklahoma Historical Society, for permission to use some of its historic photographs. I want to thank Carolyn Flood of Kingfisher for the chance to go through her large collections of images of early-day Kingfisher and for her permission to use some here, and the Kingfisher Chamber of Commerce loaned some fantastic images for use in the book.

I also want to give thanks to Mike Tautkus, director of the Kingfisher Memorial Library, for his help scanning images; Mary Haney of the Hennessey Library for information; Jim Jackson for scouring flea markets for images of Kingfisher; Tom Clark for providing access to trivia on the sports record of Kingfisher College; and Ernest Hellwege for information on the Big Four School District.

I naturally want to thank Ted Gerstle and John Pearson of Arcadia Publishing for all their help getting this project going, especially Ted, who has patiently answered all the questions that a neophyte author put to him.

Unless otherwise indicated, all images are courtesy of the Chisholm Trail Museum, Kingfisher.

INTRODUCTION

Kingfisher County lies northwest of Oklahoma City in north-central Oklahoma at the edge of the Great Plains. The 98th meridian lies just to the west of the town of Kingfisher, which is the county seat town. The other major towns in the county are Hennessey, Dover, Cashion, Okarche, and Loyal.

The Cimarron River flows roughly northwest to southeast through the middle of the county. It is a brackish river whose surface waters cannot be drunk but whose aquifer provides water for many of the towns. Turkey Creek flows from the north to enter the Cimarron River just to the west of Dover. Kingfisher lies at the intersection of Uncle John's Creek, which flows from the south, and Kingfisher Creek, which flows from the west. Kingfisher Creek was supposedly named for Nebraska rancher "King" David Fisher, who camped out along it. Early maps tend to support this theory, naming it "King Fisher's Creek." However, to be fair, there is at least one major historian who claims the creek is named after a bird.

Kingfisher Creek flows from the west of town, and just to the west of town, what is now called Winter Camp Creek (formerly known as Dead Indian Creek) joins it.

The landscape is made of gently rolling hills with not much in the way of relief, although it is not flat. Originally, it was grasslands with trees only along the creek bottoms. However, a belt of blackjack oak (*Quercus marilandica*) existed along the north side of the Cimarron River in pioneer days, although much of that has been cleared over the years.

For most of the 19th century, Oklahoma was called Indian Territory, as it was a repository for Native American tribes from all over the United States. Although the Wichita, Kiowa, Comanche, and Osage tribes are thought of as being original to Oklahoma, none of these tribes seem to have lived any length of time in Kingfisher County. In 1869, the Cheyenne and Arapaho tribes were moved here from Colorado, Wyoming, and Montana, and their reservation was established in the western portion of the county. The eastern portion of the county was called the unassigned lands, as these lands had not been given to any tribe.

In 1867, just after the end of the Civil War, a man named Joseph McCoy talked Texas ranchers into herding their longhorn cattle to sell at McCoy's stockyard in Abilene, Kansas. Later these herds were walked to other famous towns in Kansas, such as Wichita, Dodge City, Ellsworth, and Caldwell. Named for a half-Cherokee trader, Jesse Chisholm, some six million head of cattle were herded north to Kansas on the Chisholm Trail from 1867 to roughly 1887.

Starting in the 1870s, groups of settlers calling themselves boomers came to the unassigned lands trying to force them open to settlement. Led by a charismatic Indian Wars veteran named David L. Payne, their efforts eventually led to the opening of the central part of Oklahoma on April 22, 1889, in what was the first of five land runs.

In 1889, one of the two land offices where settlers registered their claims was at Kingfisher; the other was at Guthrie. J. V. Admire was receiver of monies at the land office, and J. C. Robberts was registrar of deeds.

The original bill opening Oklahoma to settlement did not allow for a town site to exceed 320 acres, so the settlers organized into two cities: Kingfisher City at the north side of the town settlement around the area of the land office (near where the old post office stood) and Lisbon to the south. Although Lisbon was larger than Kingfisher City, when the two united on June 14, 1890, the town was called Kingfisher.

The towns of Dover and Hennessey were also settled by the land run of 1889. The town of Cashion started as the town of Downs only to change its name later.

At the beginning of 1889, the Chicago, Rock Island and Pacific Railroad (Rock Island) began laying tracks south from Kansas, but it did not reach Kingfisher until October 23 of that year.

On May 2, 1890, the Organic Act created Oklahoma Territory, which consisted of the unassigned lands and the area called "No Man's Land," which was the panhandle of Oklahoma. At that time, the territory was divided into three judicial districts. The western district consisted of what is now the eastern part of Kingfisher County and Canadian County to the south and the panhandle. Missouri native Abraham Jefferson Seay was appointed judge for the western district of Oklahoma, and he chose Kingfisher as his place of residence.

The first territorial governor, George Washington Steele, laid out the outline of Kingfisher County, although he called it County Five, with Kingfisher as the county seat. Unlike other counties that have had disputes over the county seat, Kingfisher has been unchallenged since the beginning.

Kingfisher, Oklahoma City, and Guthrie competed to be chosen as territorial capital, with Oklahoma City winning at first only to be vetoed by Steele. Kingfisher then won but was also vetoed by Steele, leaving Guthrie the territorial capital by default.

Abraham Jefferson Seay was appointed the second territorial governor of Oklahoma in February 1892. Seay naturally hoped to make Kingfisher the territorial capital, but circumstances prevented him from realizing that dream. On April 19, 1892, the western portion of Kingfisher County was made available to settlement when the Cheyenne and Arapaho lands were opened by a land run. The year before, the reservation was dissolved, but each individual member of the Cheyenne or Arapaho tribe received an allotment that was 160 acres for the individual to own. The land not allotted was called surplus and was open to settlement by a land run. The town of Kiel, later called Loyal, was settled by this land run.

Kingfisher quickly became the center of a major wheat-growing area, and the Kingfisher Chamber of Commerce called the town "the Buckle of the Wheat Belt."

Kingfisher and Kingfisher County covers 1889 to the mid-1940s. It is organized by theme, yet each chapter is roughly chronological. It does not attempt to be a strict history of the county and the towns within the county but does attempt to give an overview of what the world looked like, once upon a time, in Kingfisher and Kingfisher County.

One

BEGINNINGS

Kingfisher is supposedly named for Nebraska rancher "King" David Fisher, who camped along the creek. The creek was named for him. The stage station on King Fisher Creek (later the name was combined to make Kingfisher) was a log cabin arrangement on the south side of the creek some two to three blocks west of where the old post office stood. When the eastern portion of Kingfisher County was opened by the land run of April 22, 1889, Kingfisher was the location of one of the two land offices, with J. C. Robberts as registrar of deeds and J. V. Admire as receiver of monies. The land office was not even complete when they tried to open it.

The town was originally two cities, Kingfisher City on the north and Lisbon on the south. Even though Kingfisher City was the smaller of the two communities, its name won out when the two towns were combined in June 1890. Dover was originally a trading post named Red Fork Ranch on the Old Chisholm Trail. The old name for the Cimarron River was the Red Fork of the Arkansas. Hennessy (originally spelled without the *e*) was platted near where trader Pat Hennessy was massacred by the Cheyenne and Arapaho Indians. Cashion originally started as the town of Downs and at first existed as little more than a tent stage station on the road from Guthrie to Kingfisher. Okarche stands evenly divided between Kingfisher County and Canadian County, with the line going down the middle of Main Street. It is a coined name made up from Oklahoma, Arapaho, and Cheyenne. Kiel (now Loyal), settled by the land run of 1892, stands in the northwest portion of the county and was originally named for the great German port city that lies on the Kiel shipping canal. This underscores the fact that the greatest portion of settlers in this area came from Germany. The county itself was originally County Five, quickly assuming the name Kingfisher.

This famous photograph is not that of the land run of 1889, which opened the east portion of Kingfisher County, but of the run of 1893. No photograph has yet been found of the land run of 1889.

Kingfisher started as a city of tents. The settlers were mostly men from Kansas or Missouri, carrying with them their inclination toward supporting the Republican Party, which has lasted up until the present day. A man had to be 21 years of age to take part in the run, although a single woman could stake a claim as well. A married woman was supposed to stay with her husband. (Courtesy Oklahoma Historical Society.)

Kingfisher was settled by two groups, the north liners and the west liners. The west line of the land run area was a mile west of town. People who made the run from there got better lots than those who ran from the north side of the unassigned lands. There were also two cities; the one on the north was called Kingfisher City, and the one on the south was called Lisbon. (Courtesy Oklahoma Historical Society.)

This photograph, taken the day of the run on April 22, 1889, shows some of the important men of the very beginnings of Kingfisher. Standing fourth from the left is J. V. Admire, receiver of monies at the land office, sometime mayor of Kingfisher, and founder of the *Kingfisher Times and Free Press*. J. Q. Miles, an early mayor, is standing third from the right. Sitting are Dick Crews (left) and J. C. Robberts, registrar of deeds at the Kingfisher land office. (Courtesy Carolyn Flood.)

The town of Downs was first a stage station between Kingfisher and Guthrie. The post office was established on August 12, 1889. The Chicago, Rock Island and Pacific Railroad (Rock Island) missed the town of Downs by passing to its south. So the entire town moved a half mile south on May 14, 1900. It then changed its name to Cashion for Roy Cashion, who died in the Spanish-American War. (Courtesy Oklahoma Historical Society.)

The towns of Kingfisher City and Lisbon joined in 1890 to be one city, and even though Lisbon was the larger, the name *Kingfisher* was chosen for the entire settlement. In the 1890 census, Kingfisher boasted 1,134 people. (Courtesy Carolyn Flood.)

The western half of Kingfisher County was opened by the land run of April 19, 1892. This opened up the Cheyenne and Arapaho Reservation to settlement, including the towns of Alpha and Omega and Kiel (later called Loyal). This photograph, although not labeled, could very well represent a camp of settlers waiting for that land run, or it could be a photograph of settlers waiting for the land run of 1893.

Although Kingfisher County was not settled in the land run of 1893, the line lay just north of Hennessey. These men are waiting for that land run. Hennessy was the name of the post office when it opened on July 20, 1889. The *e* was added on October 7, 1889.

By 1900, towns like Kingfisher were well established and beginning a period of steady growth and prosperity.

Two

TOWNS

Main Street of course was the street that early towns were most proud of, hoping to line it with many businesses and pave it as quickly as possible. Kingfisher, like some towns, boasted a grand courthouse, built in 1903, and, after 1913, an equally grand post office.

Impressive bank buildings lined the streets of early Kingfisher, but equally impressive private residences grew up within the town. A mile south of town, Abraham Jefferson Seay, second territorial governor of Oklahoma, built a stately Queen Anne–style house he called Horizon Hill. From the third-floor dormer window, impressive views of the growing community of Kingfisher could be seen.

Other residences included that of C. P. Wickmiller, the first druggist of Kingfisher, who built his own stately mansion. Wickmiller filled his home with Native American artifacts that have since perished.

Soon Main Street in Kingfisher was lined with houses, such as the one built by the Brownlee family, which would have done credit to any community. Smaller towns such as Dover also built comfortable homes to live in, some of which still survive in their communities.

Kingfisher and Kingfisher County grew rapidly, although they tended to plateau in the 1920s, while other cities like Enid underwent explosive growth. The county went from 8,332 in 1890 to 18,825 in 1910. Kingfisher went from 1,134 in 1890 to 2,538 in 1910. In 1910, Hennessey had grown to 1,665 people, and Okarche had 190. Kingfisher, Hennessey, Dover, Okarche, Cashion, and Loyal remain the towns in which most of the people of Kingfisher County still live.

No town made as big a change as Cashion. Starting out as Downs when the Peavine rail line, run by the Rock Island, came south of town, the whole town moved and changed its name. Here is a picture of Cashion soon after it moved, as some of the buildings are still under construction. (Courtesy Carolyn Flood.)

Here is Cashion about 1905, looking south toward the railroad depot. The Peavine rail line came from Kingfisher to the west. When the rolling stock left the east side of the railroad depot area, it belonged to the Atchison, Topeka and Santa Fe Railway (Santa Fe), and the train continued to Navina with a connection to Guthrie and on to Chandler.

16

Here is Cashion in about 1915.

The town of Kiel (later Loyal) started with the Cheyenne-Arapaho land run of 1892. It lies in the northwest portion of Kingfisher County several miles from any other town, and it looked forward to being the center of trade for a prosperous farming area. This picture is of Kiel not long after the run on April 19, 1892, as there are still some tents downtown.

The town of Hennessey received a spurt of growth after the Cherokee Outlet land run of September 16, 1893. (Courtesy Carolyn Flood.)

Kingfisher, as the county seat, pushed far ahead of the others, having 2,301 people in 1900. Here the citizens seem to be putting up a streetlight, although there are still no cars in sight. (Courtesy Kingfisher Chamber of Commerce.)

Major buildings sprang up in the town. This impressive brick building was erected in the fall of 1900 by the Anheuser-Busch Company. It housed the Farmers National Bank. Richard Pappe Sr. is the tallest of the three men near the horse and wagon at front. This building still stands as the headquarters for the Pioneer Telephone Cooperative.

This building, a mirror image of the previous although on a smaller scale, sat a block to the south. It housed the First Bank of Kingfisher, whose original wood building can be seen to its rear. It later was a jewelry store and also still stands as a small coffee shop.

The post office of Kingfisher was naturally one of the most important buildings in town. Over the years, there have been several post offices. This was the third, which stood at the intersection of Main Street and Robberts Avenue almost exactly where the original land office had been. Soon it was too small.

A new post office was started just behind the old one on October 1, 1912.

The new building was constructed by Dieter and Wenzel Construction of Joplin, Missouri, during the winter of 1912–1913.

The post office was finally completed on September 1, 1913. It remained in use until the current post office farther south was completed. The Briscoe Oil Company remodeled the interior of the building, and it stands today as the company headquarters.

Major private houses were also built in Kingfisher. Abraham Jefferson Seay, second territorial governor of Oklahoma in 1892 and 1893, built his home on the south side of town, calling in Horizon Hill. Seay sold the house in 1900, and it passed through several families until the state acquired it in 1966 and has since restored it. Here is the house as it appeared when it belonged to Ed Hockaday.

This was taken inside the tower room of the library with Lulu Marsh (left) and Nannie Sanders, nieces of Seay. Seay never married and filled the house with nieces and nephews. His sister Isabella Seay Collins served as his hostess until her death in 1900. After her death, Seay sold the mansion and moved to the Dean Hotel in what is now downtown Kingfisher.

Other important houses were built as well. This one was built by C. P. Wickmiller, the first druggist in Kingfisher. This house stood on the intersection of Eighth Street and Broadway where the tag agency now stands. Interestingly, just a block to the north, the Pappe family built a home in 1915 that was almost its exact twin. The Pappe house still stands.

C. P. Wickmiller filled the house with expensive furniture and all kinds of relics.

His most impressive collection was that of Native American artifacts from numerous tribes throughout the area. He also had an impressive collection of walking canes, some autographed by important people. Wickmiller gave his collection of Native American artifacts to Phillips University, where it perished in a fire in 1947. The cane collection survives at the Chisholm Trail Museum in Kingfisher.

Most homes were more modest. This picture was originally colored and shows that the family loved plants and like most pioneer families had a parlor piano. The father is Elihu Thomas, the mother is Lizzie, and the daughter at the piano is Hazel.

The smaller towns also built nice homes on a smaller scale. This is the Henry Hill home in Dover. Ralph and Ethel Hill are on the left with Haney and Anna Hill on the right. On the front porch is the hammock where some of the family would sleep in the summertime when it got too hot in the house.

This house, a little larger, is also in Dover.

Small towns in the country tried to build as well. Here the telephone wires have reached the town of Alpha to the northwest of Kingfisher. There were twin towns, Alpha and Omega. Omega survives.

Impressive homes were built in the country as well. This is the Schiermann family from Alpha.

Large, important homes continued to be built in Kingfisher. This was the home of the Brownlee family, built on Main Street in 1919 where the post office is currently located. This house was moved southwest of town and still stands.

The crown jewel of Kingfisher was the third courthouse, built in 1903. It dominated the Kingfisher skyline until 1959, when it was torn to the ground, supposedly because it had become structurally unsound over the years.

Three

FARMING

The earliest settlers of Kingfisher County came to the country expecting to grow the same crops as they had before in their old homes in Kansas, Iowa, Texas, and Arkansas. Corn and cotton proved not to be the best crops for Kingfisher County—that crop proved to be wheat. Kingfisher County lies at the edge of the Great Plains, and its rolling farmlands proved perfect for what is called hard red winter wheat. It is planted in the fall and harvested in the spring.

At first, each farmer had a small patch of land where he would try to grow enough for his family to survive on. Then wheat harvesting developed. It was a labor-intensive business. The land had to be plowed with a steam plow and planted, usually with horse-drawn planters. Once the wheat matured, it had to be cut by binders, also at first drawn by horse. When the wheat was cut, it was stacked in piles and threshed by large threshing machines. These machines were connected by large belts to great steam engines, which caused the machine to thresh the wheat, that is, separate the wheat from the chaff.

Many men formed threshing crews that hired out to farmers to do the work, just as today there are custom combining crews that start in Texas and work their way north as the wheat harvest develops. Nearly every 160-acre piece of land had a farm family on it, but this is a way of life that is largely a thing of the past.

Here is the homestead of Simon Peter Leitner, the man shown with his grandchildren on page 2, and his son-in-law Josiah "Barefoot" Williams. They simply have a wooden roof over what looks like a hole in the ground. (Courtesy Ginger Murphy.)

Settlers gradually built a home and a barn. This one basically has two rooms and two outbuildings. It belonged to Nellie Hopkins and J. H. Hopkins and stood east of Reeding.

Impressive homes were soon built.

This unidentified house has two stories, a huge barn, and a picket gate.

This handsome two-story house belonged to the Stanley family, who lived near the town of Alpha northwest of Kingfisher.

This house was on the Vieth farm east of Kingfisher. The Vieths went on to own an implement store in Kingfisher and took a prominent role in Kingfisher development. Richard Pappe of another prominent family is in the horse and buggy.

At first, farmers planted the same as they had back home. This cornfield was on the Sutton farm. While corn is still grown in Kingfisher County, usually in home gardens, it has never been as important here as it has been in some other states. (Courtesy Kingfisher Chamber of Commerce.)

As cotton was grown all over the south, it was tried here too. Dover, for a time, had a cotton gin like many other towns in Oklahoma. However, cotton was never important in Kingfisher County, and although *The Oklahoma Red Book* of 1913 gives statistics for cotton harvesting in other counties, it lists no poundage at all for Kingfisher County. This cotton was on the Jennings farm. (Courtesy Kingfisher Chamber of Commerce.)

Here is a banner load of cotton on the George King farm. The meaning of the reversed flag is unknown, but flag etiquette in the early days was not as strict as it is today. (Courtesy Kingfisher Chamber of Commerce.)

Hard red winter wheat became the prominent crop, almost to the point of being a monoculture. In the early days, the plowing was done by steam tractors and was very labor intensive. (Courtesy Kingfisher Chamber of Commerce.)

The workhorse was the steam tractor. It was connected to the other machines doing the work by a series of belts and pulleys, which could be quite dangerous. This steam tractor belonged to Henry Stetler.

An average day's cutting was 12 to 15 acres, but 20 acres could be cut on a really big day.

The threshing machine threshed the stacked bundles of wheat. This picture is dated 1915 and shows Preston Trindle at front on the engine and William Alexander Trindle at rear on the separator. Others in the crew were also of the Trindle family.

Here the smoke is coming from the steam engine, and in the background, the threshed wheat is being thrown into the air. A full crew was about 20 men using five bundles or hayracks. A big day's threshing was 300 bushels.

This photograph is from the Cashion area and shows the Stalder family. The belts on the machines are quite clearly connected. It also shows that threshing is something participated in by the entire family. Threshing started in July and could last all summer.

Here they have had to tear down part of an old-fashioned wood paling fence to get to the wheat that needs to be threshed.

Here the wheat is being neatly stacked into the square bales, which were used until very recently, when the shortage of baling wire led to the use of the large, round bales that are more common today. In the background, the building with the spire is Parker Hall, the main administration building of Kingfisher College, which places this picture just to the east of Kingfisher sometime between about 1900 and 1920.

The horses and the men that were in the field all day pulled out a cook shack in which the women cooked a large lunch and sometimes supper for the threshing crew.

Farmers were naturally interested in the latest equipment. Here the Ed Hockaday Company has an outdoor display showing some of the latest farm equipment. Ed Hockaday came to Kingfisher in 1889 and eventually owned 14 stores.

All of these binders were sold in 1916 by Kingfisher hardware store owner Josiah Gooden. He invited farmers to assemble their horses and machines on Main Street in front of the Gooden store. Fred Karrenbrock is on the binder at the front.

40

The raising of cattle is still very important in Kingfisher. These steers, nicknamed Tom, Dick, and Harry, supposedly weighed 3,715, 3,410, and 3,100 pounds, respectively, and belonged to Joe Grimes. Although some swear that they were as big as this postcard claims, close inspection of the card shows that this is probably an early-day version of "Photoshopping." (Author's collection.)

Here Tom and Dick are yoked together, making what was claimed to be the biggest yoke of cattle ever. (Author's collection.)

Even if one's cattle were not as big as Tom, Dick, or Harry, a person still wanted to take them to town, show them off, and hopefully sell them. This cattle fair was at Cashion on September 14 and 15, 1916.

Some years, the farmers had bumper crops too big to fill the elevators. The wheat then spilled out onto the ground. This bumper crop dates to about 1940.

The object was to take wheat to the mill and have it ground into flour or stored in an elevator until it could be shipped to markets elsewhere. The Kingfisher Mill and Elevator Company was on the east side of the railroad tracks where the Burrus elevator later stood.

Every town of any size had its mill.

These freight cars are at Hennessey about 1899.

The ultimate goal was to ship the wheat to markets elsewhere. The Rock Island built a north–south line through Kingfisher, which reached the town in the fall of 1889.

Four

MAKING A LIVING

Some settlers came to the area to take up jobs they had in their old hometowns or start new jobs that they had always wanted to attempt. The contractors, builders, carpenters, and lumberyards were busy as the new towns were built. As lumber was scarce on the prairies, the railroads brought it in along with the paint, nails, tools, and other items needed to construct the new cities. Although slow at first, highways and bridges strengthened the towns' connection with the outside world. If one did visit a town but did not have a relative or friend to stay with, hotels were available. The people of larger cities like Kingfisher prided themselves on having a large hotel where people could stay, although the size of the hotels in towns like Hennessey was not far behind.

A blacksmith served not just to shoe the horses or mules but also to shape the various metal items needed on an individual basis. The machine shop grew up, operated by gigantic belts to turn the lathes. The towns' people had small plots to grow some food but needed grocery stores. The supermarket had not been invented, but there was the meat market and the canned goods store. The main street of Kingfisher at one time had several individual grocery stores. Drugstores were needed as were men's and women's clothing stores, banks, barbershops, confectioneries (early-day ice-cream parlors), restaurants, ice plants, and all the other businesses needed for a small town. A good fire department was needed early on, as so many of the buildings were wood, often still lit by kerosene. Looking at the images of these businesses brings back an age not so far away in time but compared to the modern age of super chain stores, it is one vastly different in spirit.

Of course, one of the main ways of making a living in the early days was construction. This is Charles E. Sockler, builder of the courthouse, seen here constructing something else in Kingfisher.

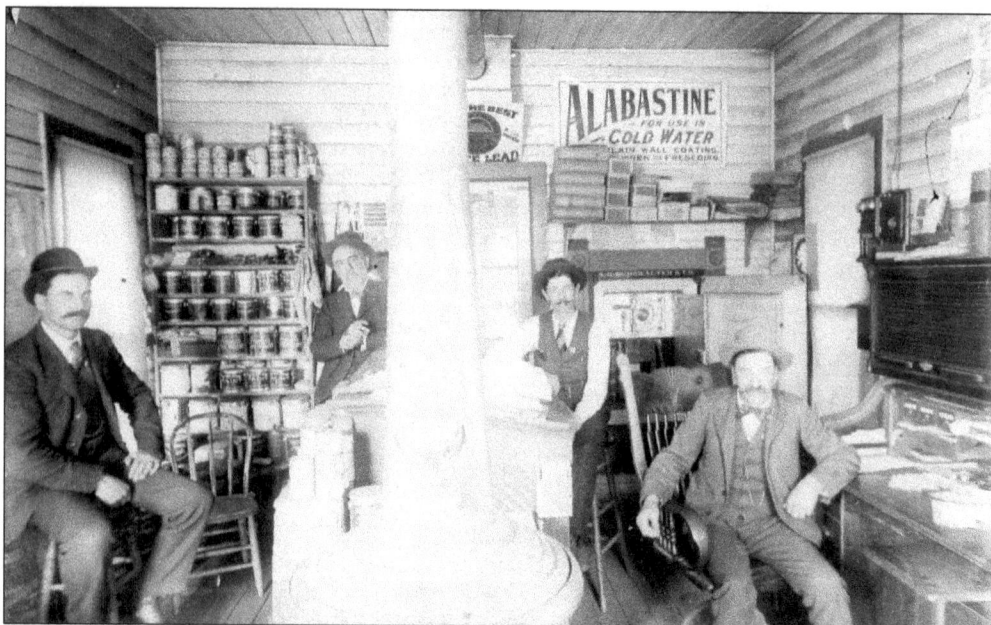

Lumberyards did a big business. Here is the Schowalter lumberyard in Kingfisher, owned by A. H. Schowalter. It stood roughly where Tom's Drug stands today. A. H. Ruth is seated on the left.

Seen in the center is the drugstore of C. P. Wickmiller, with Wickmiller in the front door of the store. This was the first two-story building in Kingfisher.

Before statehood and Prohibition arrived, in 1907, Kingfisher had over a dozen saloons. Here Richard Pappe combines a saloon and a bakery, because the yeast of the flour makes good beer.

Here is the Kingfisher Fire Department of 1905. The horses are Dan (left) and Joe. On the wagon are, from left to right, Fire Chief Andy Woods, George Hart, George Brown, Barney Eakins, "Doc" Linder, Sam Alexander, Clem Thorne, George Long, Frank Coke, and Bob Christian. When one of the horses of the original team died, the other horse would not work with its replacement.

This is the engine called "Old Huldy," which worked the branch railroad that went from Kingfisher to Cashion, Cashion to Navina, and later on through Chandler. The line was nicknamed the Peavine. The Guthrie-to-Chandler branch ended in 1923, the Cashion-to-Navina line ended in 1931, and the Kingfisher-to-Cashion branch ended in 1935. (Author's collection.)

Every small town had to have its railroad station. This is the one for Dover. (Courtesy Oklahoma Historical Society.)

C. R. I. & P. R. R. STATION, KINGFISHER, OKLA.
Smith Photo 122

KINGFISHER

Here is the railroad station for Kingfisher.

The blacksmith shop in town was very important. Here is J. S. Robison of Dover, a blacksmith and general handyman.

The machine shop was important as well. Oftentimes many of the lathes were operated by large pullies, like this one in Kingfisher. The owners of the machine shop are not identified, although the picture belonged to the Stetler family.

The Kingfisher Ice Plant was set on the east side of town next to Uncle John's Creek and the swinging bridge that connected the town to the park on the other side of the creek. The ice plant built a dam at the bridge to impound water for use in the plant.

Grocery stores filled Main Street in downtown Kingfisher as late as the early 1950s. This one sat on the east side of the street across from the old post office next to the Anheuser-Busch building.

Building the roads and bridges that led in and out of Kingfisher provided jobs for many. The man in the front is the contractor, C. E. Sockler. The man in the cap is his son Charles Sockler. The two girls are Violet Sockler Southwick (left) and Rose Sockler Kooken.

This is the Hauser meat market in Kingfisher at Christmas, sometime between 1912 and 1914. It sat in the 200 block on the east side of Main Street.

This is the Robertson grocery store, probably in the 1920s, with Dove Meade in the white hat.

The interior of the Wickmiller drugstore, seen here in the 1920s or 1930s, seems like a magic cavern.

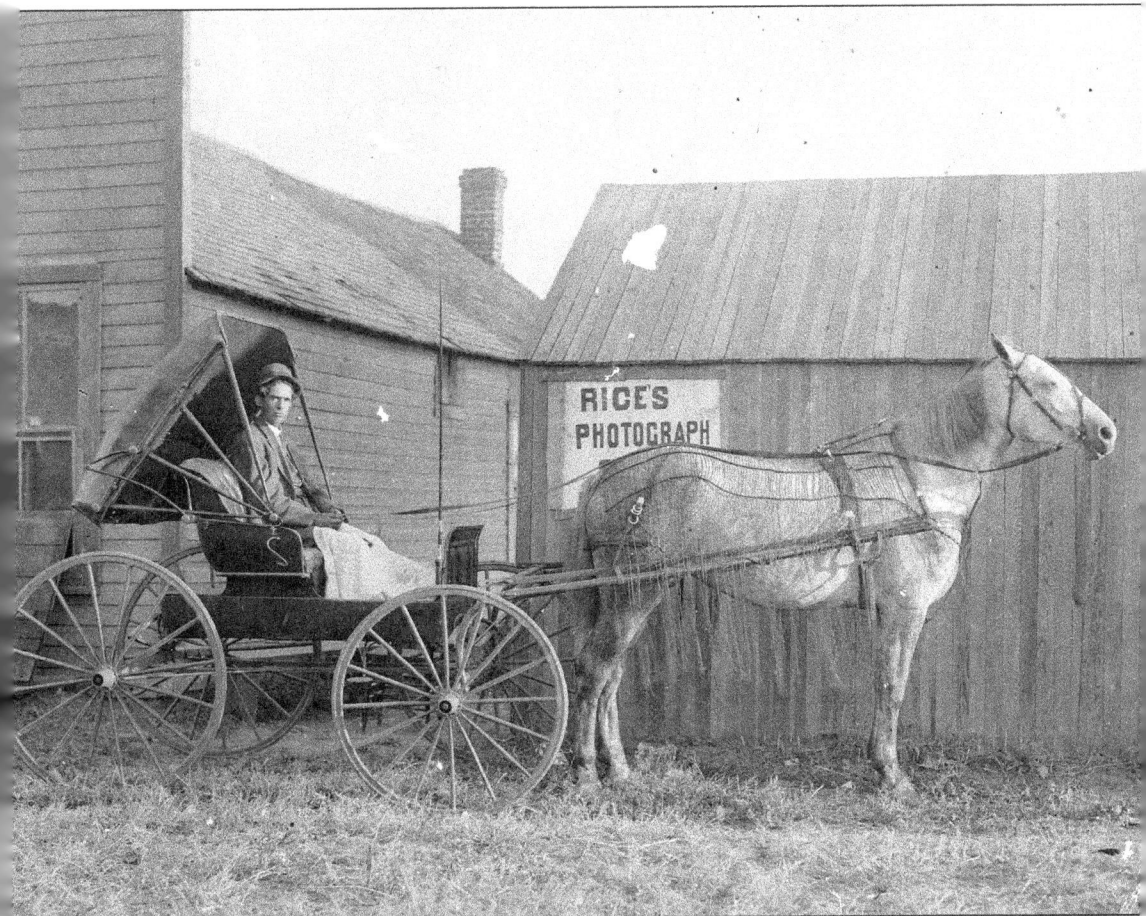

Photographers came to every corner of Kingfisher County. As this photograph is of Hugh Trosper of Kiel, the photographer's shop was probably in that town as well.

Other small towns had businesses that were also important. Here is the creamery for Okarche. (Courtesy Oklahoma Historical Society.)

The stores in smaller towns tended to be more like general stores. The Dover Cash Store advertises that it has a meat market and ice. The building still stands on the west side of the little that is left of Dover's main street, although the store has been empty for years.

This oil well dates to around 1914 and was on the William Burns farm near Dover.

As important as oil is at the present time in Kingfisher, it never really took off until the 1940s. Here is an attempt to find oil near Kiel in the early 1920s.

Specialty stores developed in the bigger towns like Kingfisher. Here is the men's clothing store. In the picture are, from left to right, ? Crutchfield, Roger Provine, and Grady Meade.

Here is Little Joe's Confectionary, which stood in the 200 block on Main Street in Kingfisher. Jack Cannoy is in the middle.

In addition to being teachers, women were telephone switchboard operators. This is Lula Shaw at the telephone. At present, Kingfisher is the home for Pioneer Telephone Cooperative, the largest cooperatively owned telephone company west of the Mississippi River.

Banks were naturally important. Here Elmer Solomon is the cashier. The bank counter looks very much like the one preserved in the bank building in the little village at the rear of the Chisholm Trail Museum, which is housed in what was the first bank building of Kingfisher.

Hotels were at the center of town. This is the Rhodes Hotel in Hennessey, which stood at the corner of Oklahoma Avenue and Cherokee Street. The people standing in front include Perry Mathews, Walter Cupps, and Dr. E. D. Bradley. It burned down in 1921, killing four people.

Many images exist of the Kingfisher Hotel, built in 1892. It stood in what is now an empty parking lot just to the east of the *Kingfisher Times and Free Press* building. The interior pictures on pages 61 and 62 were taken by Dick McConkey, who was a prominent photographer in Enid for many years.

Here is an interior shot of the dining room of the Kingfisher Hotel.

❋ SUNDAY DINNER ❋

....AT....

Hotel Kingfisher.

W. G. BRISTOW, Proprietor.

Oyster Soup
New York Counts   Select Celery   Queen Olives
Baked Mackinaw Trout
Boiled Pickled Ox Tongue   Boiled Winchester Ham

Prime Sirloin of Beef, au Jus
Roast Turkey, Cranberry Sauce   Teal Duck, with Mushrooms
Roast Pork with Apple Sauce

Fricassed Giblets
Macaroni a la Frasia   Boston Cream Buffs, Crested
Green Apple Fritters, Wine Sauce
Calves Brains, Chartula

Mashed Cream Potatoes   Lima Beans   Lady Peas
Stewed Tomatoes

English Punch   Wisconsin Creamery Cheese
Minced Apple Roll   Lemon Ice Cream   Peach Pie
Lemon Pie
Nuggets of Fruit   Assorted Cake
Iced Tea   Coffee   Iced Milk

Kingfisher, Oklahoma, Sunday, October 16, 1898.

The menu for Sunday, October 16, 1898, has been preserved.

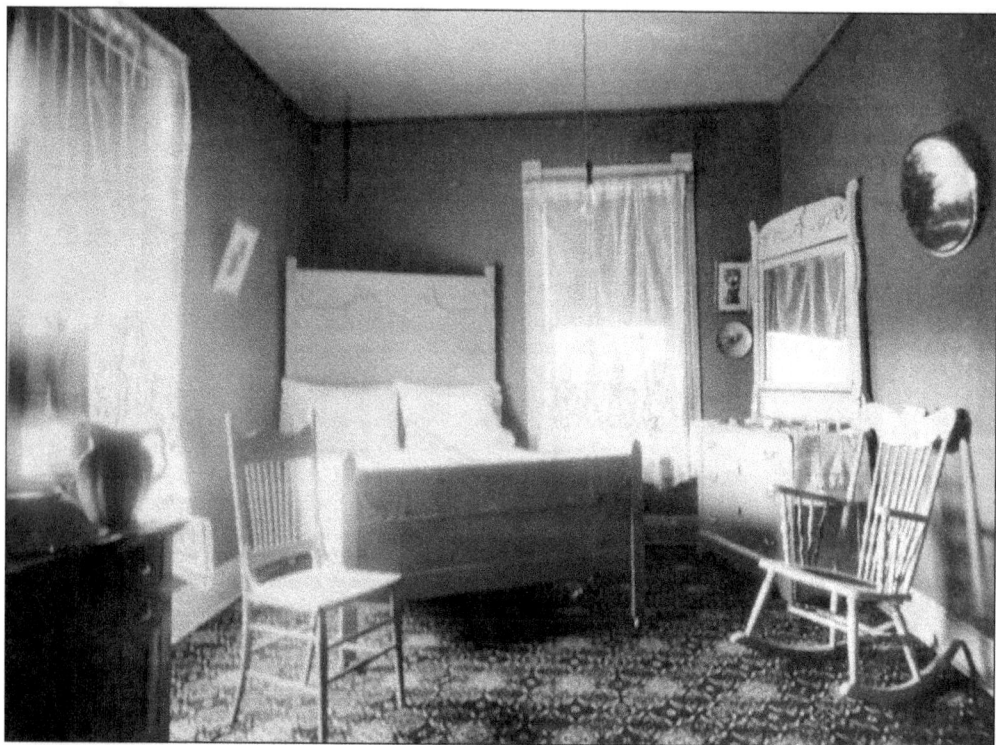

This is a fine interior picture of one of the bedrooms.

The Kingfisher Hotel had its own barbershop. This picture dates to about 1914, and Jack Cannoy is in the barber's chair.

It was not too long before owning an automobile dealership was an important way of making a living. This one dates to about 1910 and is probably the dealership of M. O. Stetler, the first automobile dealership in Kingfisher.

Model Ts were soon filling up the main streets of America, including in Kingfisher.

Many fond memories survive of these early businesses and the people who worked in them. This is a picture of an unidentified cashier in the Roberts drugstore in Dover.

Five

CHURCHES

The religious life of the early settlers was very important. At first, the settlers in the country had Sunday services in individual homes, and it was only later that small country churches appeared. In towns like Kingfisher, the various denominations had Sunday services as soon as possible, from the back of a buckboard if necessary. As soon as any money could be scraped together, they established a church building. Many of the settlers came from Kansas and brought their denominations with them. They were primarily Disciples of Christ (Christian Church) and Methodists. Baptists were prominent among the settlers from Texas and Arkansas. As Kingfisher County was heavily settled by people of German and Czech descent, the churches they brought with them reflected that background. In Okarche, the Lutheran and Catholic Churches were both so strong that they could have their own parish schools. The Czechs were strongly Catholic. In addition, many people of German descent belonged to the Evangelical and Reformed Churches. During the World War I, many members of this congregation faced discrimination as church services were still held in German. It would not be until after the war that they, very reluctantly, decided to worship in English. The Presbyterian Church and the Congregational Church also had a presence in the territory. There were smaller churches, such as the Pentecostal Holiness Churches and the Assembly of God Churches. The black community had its own separate churches, with the African Methodist Episcopal Church being important. Each of these churches played a large role not only in the spiritual life of the towns but also in their social and educational developments.

Religion has always been an important part of life in Kingfisher and Kingfisher County. Many people came to Kingfisher to start a new life both physically and spiritually. The beginning of this life, according to Christian doctrine, is baptism into the faith. Many churches believe that baptism should be by complete immersion. As few churches existed with the facilities for immersion, it would take place at a river, creek, or farm pond. This baptism took place on Easter, April 23, 1916, probably in a creek east of Reeding.

Every small community had its own little church. Here is the Beulah church at Altona in southeastern Kingfisher County.

The Park Congregational Church lay west of Kingfisher. This building was completed in the fall of 1894 and used until July 1962. The church was small and struggling, so when the Congregational Church joined with the Evangelical and Reformed denominations to form the United Church of Christ, members of this church joined with the one in Kingfisher to become part of the Federated Church. This picture dates to 1911.

The two churches on this page appear to be identical, but closer inspection reveals that they are not. This one appears to be the Evangelical Church of Dover. This building survives as a private residence.

This church is the Disciples of Christ (Christian) Church of Kingfisher. The structure was dedicated on December 31, 1891. The current structure was dedicated on April 13, 1930.

In German, the sign on the church reads, "German Evangelical Peace Church, 1902." This congregation met together with the Lutherans until the Lutheran church was built in 1905. This is the old Evangelical and Reformed church at the corner of Eighth Street and Sheridan Avenue. It is now the home of Marvin and Irene Reames.

CONGREGATIONAL CHURCH, KINGFISHER, OKLA.
Smith Photo 125

Not all denominations made a go of it in the new territory. The Congregational Church, with its strong ties to New England, at first seemed to have the advantage over other churches, but in many cases, these church families did not survive. The Kingfisher Congregational Church later joined with the Methodists.

The strong German background of the county insured that there would be a strong representation of German Catholics in the community. This is the Catholic church of Kingfisher. The parish started with a small frame structure built in 1892 and dedicated to St. Anne. The parish grew so fast that a bigger church was needed. This is the current church dedicated to SS. Peter and Paul. Its cornerstone was laid on August 22, 1903. (Author's collection.)

The photograph is identified as the Congregational Church of Okarche.

This is the Disciples of Christ church in Dover, established in 1907. This building still exists.

The church was an important part for much of the social life of the community. This unidentified church group is probably trying to re-create the dress of the beginning of the Bible school program of a denomination.

One of the goals of any church was a solid, substantial building that not only glorified God but also showed that the church family had succeeded in the new community. The Methodist Church of Kingfisher was built in 1917 and still stands at the intersection of Main Street and Broadway. (Courtesy Carolyn Flood.)

Six

SCHOOLS

Both the settlers in the countryside and the settlers in the towns recognized the importance of education. In the land run of 1889, they set aside two sections, 16 and 36, as school lands. That is, settlers leased the lands, and the money went for the upkeep of the schools. By 1907, the school lease money amounted to several thousand dollars a day for the entire new state of Oklahoma.

The very first schools were subscription schools; farmers in the area or people in town raised the money to pay a teacher. The teacher could be a man or a single woman, especially since married women were not supposed to be separate from their husbands. Later school boards were organized, and the people of a community pitched in to help build proper schoolhouses. These schoolhouses often served as community centers for the surrounding area.

The county offered what were called normal schools, a time (probably during the summer) when all the teachers in the county went together to learn what they were supposed to be teaching. In the country, schools were usually grades one through six and rarely to grade eight. Students got a certificate showing that they had completed the six grades worth of work offered at their schools. Early on in cities like Kingfisher, Okarche, Dover, and Hennessey, provisions were made for a high school, although not many students from the countryside were able to take advantage of it. Kingfisher had grander ambitions. It decided to start a college, Kingfisher College, for those fortunate students who were able to go beyond the high school level in their educations.

Schools were important to early settlers. Just as the provisions for the territory set up the mechanism for supporting schools, every area worked hard to get the schools going. In theory, every country school was about three miles apart. This sod school dates to about 1902 and is the East Willard Subscription School near Cashion, with the Reverend Frank Hamand as teacher.

Wandel was 10 miles to the northeast of Kingfisher and was a post office from May 5, 1890, to March 15, 1904. This picture dates to 1893, and E. S. McCabe is the teacher. McCabe worked both in the Hennessey school system and at Kingfisher. Wandel later became part of the Big Four School District.

In the summer, the counties offered normal schools, which were schools for the teachers to learn what they needed to know to teach the students. Here is the Kingfisher normal school for 1895. The building sat roughly where the Disciples of Christ church sits today.

The Mound Ridge School sat northwest of Kingfisher. This dates to 1908. Some of the students pictured include Ernest Kirsch, Walt Meier, Anna Storm, Bernice Burrus, and George Struck. The first on the left in the third row is Will Storm, who lost his life in World War I. The teacher is Emmet Patterson.

The larger towns naturally had a larger school system. This is a picture of the students of Okarche.

Some country schools had substantial structures. This is the district 84 school (Plainview), northwest of Kingfisher, with a Miss Way as teacher. The flag is pre-1907. (Courtesy Kingfisher Chamber of Commerce.)

This Hennessey High School building was constructed in 1894. This postcard dates to before 1913, as that was when the building was remodeled and the cupola removed.

Kingfisher, the biggest city in the county, had the largest school system. This building was erected in 1898 and originally served all the grade levels. When the new high school was constructed at the south edge of town in 1911, it served as the grade school until 1933. Then the building was demolished and Washington Grade School took its place.

Here is E. S. McCabe, who served as superintendent of the Kingfisher school system from about 1904 to 1916.

This companion piece of the interior of a classroom at Kingfisher was probably taken at the same time, possibly in 1911 when the new high school building was opened.

In 1911, the new high school was built at what was then the south side of town. In 1921, just to the south of it, another large school was constructed, and this building served as the junior high. It is no longer standing.

Here is the Kingfisher High School girls' basketball team of 1904. The starters were Lulu Brown and Fannie Hoyt. The guards were Pearl Shaw and Harriett White, with Kate Hoyt, Celia Tett, and Blanche Pratt as forwards. The substitute was Inez Tish. Ernest Preston was the coach.

These are Kingfisher High School students, probably in front of the old building, so it is before 1911.

Kingfisher also boasted a small four-year liberal arts college named Kingfisher College. Founded as an academy in 1894, it grew to be housed in several buildings on College Hill, one mile east of town. This is Parker Hall, named after J. H. Parker, the founder of Kingfisher College. It became the administration building. His daughter Harriet Parker Camden wrote "Oklahoma, a Toast," which was the first state song. (Author's collection.)

Kingfisher College had three men accepted to be Rhodes scholars. The man on the left is Ray Lange. The other Rhodes scholars were Charlie Mahaffie and Claude Vogt, who did not finish his time at Oxford University due to poor health. Lange's tennis partner is Earl Mick.

Kingfisher College remains in trivia books, because in 1917, its football team lost to the University of Oklahoma 179-0, which is the highest point score accumulated by the university. Most of the time, the team was not that bad, playing the University of Oklahoma to a scoreless tie in 1903 and playing what is now Oklahoma State University to a scoreless tie in 1906. The two men pictured are Jack P. Dwight and Alley Porter.

The life of the college was cut short when it closed in 1922. The depression at the end of World War I crippled its finances. The trustees of the college invested in a flour mill in town that was owned by one of the board members of the college. When the flour mill folded, the college went with it. The buildings were later used by the Pentecostal Holiness Church that formed King's College. In 1932, it too closed.

Some country schools continued to flourish. This is Omega in the 1930s. The Omega school system and the Loyal school system combined to form the Lomega school system in 1968. The town of Omega still exists, although its twin, Alpha, has long since vanished.

As early as the 1920s, many of the small country school districts saw that they would have to consolidate to survive. On March 17, 1920, district 64, Whitecap; district 65, Twilight; district 71, Wandel; and district 72, Bird Creek, came together to form the Big Four School District that did not finally close until 1978. This is the Big Four grade school band in the mid-1940s.

The impact of the teachers on the lives of the students was, of course, enormous. Many of the teachers became prominent individuals in the community in their own right. Here is Lee Boecher, a teacher in Alpha. Boecher wrote a book titled *Short Grass Country* about his experiences as a teacher.

The figure of the schoolteacher remains an icon to this day. This is Della Packard Cushing of Hennessey.

Seven

PEOPLE

Kingfisher and Kingfisher County were settled primarily by people of German and Czech descent, so names like Boeckman, Bredel, Jech, Vieth, Fiegel, or Grabow give a different look to the telephone directory than some other places.

The western portion of the county was originally the Cheyenne and Arapaho Reservation. When that reservation was dissolved by the land run of 1892, each member of the two tribes was allowed to take an allotment of land to own. In the case of the Cheyenne and Arapaho Indians, the allotments were 160 acres and were usually located along the creeks and the rivers within the reservation. Many of these allotments remain in the various Native American families, even if they do not live on their property. They lease these lands to farmers on a long-term basis.

Kingfisher County also had a sizable population of black settlers. A black man or a single black woman could make the land run and stake a claim just like anyone else. The bulk of the black population came in the land run of 1892, and many of their ancestors still live in Kingfisher and Dover.

Military service has been important to the people of Kingfisher County. Roy Cashion of Hennessey was the first person from Oklahoma Territory to die on foreign soil. He died on July 1, 1898, on the charge up San Juan Hill.

The people naturally are the core of what makes up Kingfisher and Kingfisher County.

After 1868, many Cheyenne and Arapaho Indians lived only a mile west of Kingfisher on their reservation. From left to right are (first row) Elliot Tasso, Andrew Tasso, Gilbert Tasso, Lena Tasso, Lizzie Foote, an unidentified boy, Gilbert Foote, George Pedigo, and a dog; (second row) Luther Altizer, Nettie Tasso, Mary Tasso, Anne Pedigo, Eva Tasso, ? Rhoades, and Mina Rhoades.

Here is a Native American encampment from west of Hennessey in 1900.

Cheyenne and Arapaho Indians were a common sight on Kingfisher's Main Street. From left to right, these young ladies are Evelyn Black, born in 1908; Caroline Black, born in 1914; and Mary Black, born in 1905. Given Caroline Black's appearance, the picture is from about 1920.

This is prominent Cheyenne Indian
Sampson Kelley.

Fighting Bull is in the center of the photograph, taken looking to the north of the water tower
in the parking lot behind Schowalter's lumber store that later became the Safeway store and is
now Tom's Drug Store.

Young Cheyenne and Arapaho Indian men attended the Carlisle Indian School in Carlisle, Pennsylvania, both to learn a trade and to try to become acculturated to the American way of life. Few teachers of that time had any respect for Native American language and traditions and often did everything they could to eliminate any traces of the past. This young man is unidentified.

The Cheyenne and Arapaho people maintain a strong presence in Kingfisher and Kingfisher County even today. This is Jerome and Pansy Thomas from about 1944.

Although black people made the land run of 1889, the bulk of them came to take part in the run of 1892. A strong black contingent exists both in the city of Kingfisher and a community to the east of Dover. This man was from Dover, and the picture is dated January 20, 1937. He is only identified as Mr. Taylor.

"Apostle" Paul Sykes was born a slave in Grenada, Mississippi, in March 1842. He came to Kingfisher in 1891.

Sykes became famous for his visits to the Rock Island depot where he danced and sang for loose change to help support his Straight Gate Church, which he started in 1898. He sang his own composition, "Old Ark's a Moverin."

Although Sykes became well known in Kingfisher, he died in poverty on October 1, 1929. Finally in 1957, a gravestone was erected for him by people who remembered the work he did and his song.

The young men about town joined clubs both for the enjoyment and to get their names before the public. It is not known what club or special event these young men of Kingfisher are dressed up for, and not all their names have been preserved, but Elmer Solomon is the first on the left in the second row, and Harley T. Davis is the first on the right in the first row. The two men were brothers-in-law and later became business partners.

Young men in Hennessey dressed up as well to show their prosperity. Each seems to have a cigar. Roy Cashion's brother Arthur Cashion is on the left in the third row.

Some men came to Kingfisher to enter politics. This is Abraham Jefferson Seay, the second territorial governor of Oklahoma. He came to Kingfisher in 1890 to be a territorial judge and was appointed governor in October 1891. Seay was appointed by Pres. Benjamin Harrison, a Republican who lost the election of 1892, so he only served as governor until the spring of 1893. Seay lived in Kingfisher until near the end of his life and is buried here.

J. V. Admire came from Kansas to be receiver of monies at the Kingfisher land office. In 1890, Admire and his friends tried unsuccessfully to get him appointed as the first territorial governor. Admire made his mark as the editor of the *Kingfisher Times and Free Press* newspaper, which survives today. This is Admire and the first white child born in Oklahoma Territory, Admire Lewis. Admire won an auction to name the child with a bid of $52.50 dollars.

Joining the military has always been important to many men from Kingfisher County. This is E. C. Hill in his World War I uniform.

This parade of navy men also seems to date to World War I.

The first man from Oklahoma Territory to die on foreign soil was Roy Cashion of Hennessey, who died on July 1, 1898, in the charge up San Juan Hill during the Spanish-American War. His body was returned after four and a half years, and a funeral procession took place in Hennessey on January 30, 1903. Cashion was buried in the Hennessey cemetery.

This is a Spanish-American War caisson such as was used in the military funerals of this time.

By the 1920s, the people of Kingfisher and Kingfisher County counted themselves as sophisticated and up-to-date as anyone in the country. Here are Court Pappe Sr. and Mary Drake Pappe about 1924.

One man who made a considerable impression on the Midwest was Joseph Danne (1887–1959). Although self-taught, Danne experimented with different strains of wheat to make them more drought resistant and more resistant to insects. He developed the Triumph and Super-Triumph wheat that were used throughout the Midwest and are still the basis for many of the strains of wheat used today. Here Danne (right) is receiving an award for his work.

Eight

DISASTERS

It might have seemed a good idea at the time to build Kingfisher at the intersection of Kingfisher Creek and Uncle John's Creek, but over the years, these creeks have produced many floods that have impacted the lives of residents.

To the north, Turkey Creek flows south from Enid until it intersects with the Cimarron River to the southwest of Dover. When Turkey Creek overflows, Dover floods. The Cimarron River flows through the county roughly from the northwest to its south-central portion. Rainstorms farther west occasionally fill the river, and the resulting floods can cut the county in half. In earlier days, it was the railroad bridge that was cut and later it was the highway.

Kingfisher County is also in the middle of tornado alley. What early settlers called Kansas cyclones turned out to be just as numerous in Oklahoma. The most recent large outbreak of tornados was in 1999, which killed one person in Dover. Fires were a frequent occurrence, often destroying courthouses with precious records or a church that a congregation had worked hard to build. Then there are disasters peculiar to wheat elevators, when the wheat dust ignites and explodes. This continues to happen even today. The people of Kingfisher County faced all these and more and managed to overcome them all.

When the two creeks flood, they fill the whole northwestern and often northeastern part of town. This is probably a picture of the great flood of 1912 showing the west bottom flooded with what looks like the spire of the Christian church in the background.

Uncle John's Creek on the east side of town filled up as well. Here is a picture probably from the flood of 1908. This shows Uncle John's Creek up over the swinging bridge, which was built to allow entrance to the park on the east side of town.

During floods, Kingfisher Creek cuts off the north side of town, nowadays cutting off U.S. Highway 81 going to the north. This photograph is dated May 8, 1912. The unfinished post office is just off the edge of the photograph to the left.

This photograph was probably taken at the exact same time as the previous picture, with the camera swung to the right to show the businesses being affected by the flood. If the photographer had swung a little more to the right, he would have photographed the Anheuser-Busch building. This area still floods.

Turkey Creek, just to the west of Dover, also floods as it pours from the north to enter the Cimarron River to the southwest of town. Here is Dover during a flood, possibly in 1912.

Here is another photograph of Dover during a flood with people up on boxcars to see the extent of the damage.

Floodwaters in front of the post office were a common sight. This is probably the flood of 1942.

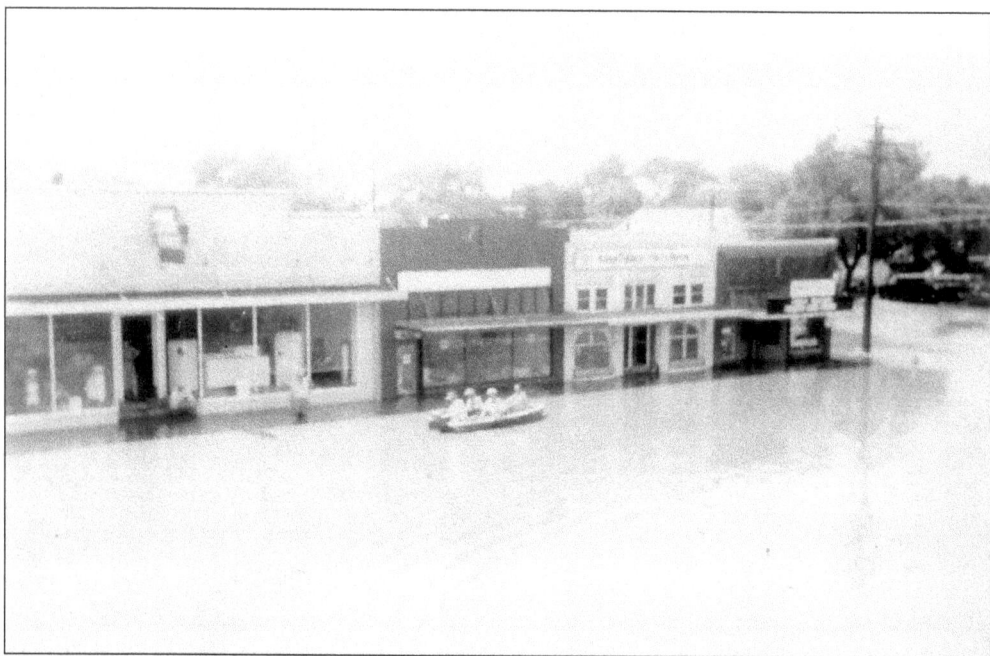

This is of the same flood, a little farther to the right from the image above.

The flood with the most memorable consequences was that of September 18, 1906. The Cimarron River flooded and undermined the supports of the railroad bridge.

The train drove onto the bridge just as the supports gave way, and the train crashed into the river.

The crash became notorious. Some newspaper reports said that several hundred had died, claiming bodies were found miles downstream. A news notice closer to the accident claimed that two died and 25 were missing. The exact number of dead remains unknown. This view is from the south side of the river showing the wreckage of the mail coach.

Some newspapers claimed that the railroad company delayed putting up another replacement bridge, and when it finally did, it was substandard. Here workers are making a start on the new bridge.

Here is what looks like the completed new bridge. Some accounts say that the railroad company used the train's locomotive as one of the supports of the new bridge. A more likely account says that the supports of the new bridge are so close to the locomotive that it can never be retrieved from the river bottom. The bell of the train, however, was salvaged.

On May 23, 1909, a tornado destroyed the Victory School in district 75, called the brick school. The brick school was replaced by a frame building, and school was held there until March 1917. Pictured are, from left to right, (first row) Agnes, Catherine, Henry, Mary, and Anna Vorderlandwehr; (second row) Henry Danne, John, Gertrude, and Philomena Vorderlandwehr, Mary Danne, Charles Vorderlandwehr, and Joe Danne.

A fire destroyed the Hennessey Christian Church on January 22, 1911. Here the ladies of the congregation are gathering up bricks from the old church that could be used for rebuilding. (Courtesy Oklahoma Historical Society.)

A tornado also came through Hennessey. This picture is from around 1912, as the old Hennessey High School with its cupola can be seen in the background. This cupola was remodeled in 1913.

This is a photograph of the destruction of the Crawford family's barn at Hennessey, dating to around 1912.

On February 14, 1940, a huge boom was heard, announcing that the head house of the Burrus elevator had just exploded. Marvin Anglin was killed by the falling concrete, and three others were injured.

The bins in the elevator that were full of wheat were not damaged, but the empty ones were broken a good part of the way down. It took several months to fix the sides and put on a new bin and head house. The explosion was caused by wheat dust spontaneously igniting, an accident that still happens from time to time in grain elevators across the Midwest.

This photograph of Kingfisher Creek during the flood of 1948 was taken by George Brownlee for the *Kingfisher Times and Free Press*. In an attempt to lessen the effects of flooding, the creek was straightened in the mid-1950s. However, flooding continues. Upstream flood control on Uncle John's Creek reduced flooding on the east side of town, but Kingfisher Creek continues to flood badly, with the most recent flood being in 2007.

Nine

AT PLAY

From the beginning, settlers knew the importance of play in their lives, no matter what form it took. In May 1889, the founders of Kingfisher set aside a park for the use of their citizens, which exists to this day. The activities took a variety of forms. Nearly every little town had a baseball team, and rivalries between the towns were as serious as professional sports today. These teams were organized by adults, as it was only later that high school athletics came to dominate the sports activities of a town.

Many small towns had bands, and the central parks of the towns had bandstands on which these bands could play. The Fourth of July was always a good excuse to have a parade, although fair days were important also. Fair days gave farmers the excuse to bring their produce to the city to show off how successful they were and to see the latest farm equipment that would hopefully improve their lives. Even the dawn of the 20th century saw Santa Claus come to Dover, no doubt bringing presents, however small, that the children treasured. During the 1920s and 1930s, the movies and then radio came along to fill the time, but before then, card games, sitting on the porch, or riding in the country seemed to fill the need for play and leave one with a nostalgic feeling of a time long gone.

The settlers of Kingfisher saw the importance of having a park from the beginning. On the east side of town, Uncle John's Creek makes a small curve that outlines the perfect area for a park. So in May 1889, it was set aside as a park. They erected a suspension bridge to enter it, and the swinging bridge remains to this day. (Courtesy Kingfisher Chamber of Commerce.)

Balloon ascensions were offered in Kingfisher. This is not in the park, as there is a private home in the background.

After World War I, barnstorming became popular. This biplane is getting ready to offer rides. This photograph was taken in 1919 or 1920.

The Fourth of July was very important. Here is Main Street in Kingfisher with young boys involved in a footrace.

Santa Claus found his way to the H. B. Harnar store in Dover about 1904.

Many small towns had bands. Here is the Cashion Concert Band. From left to right are (first row) Harry Calhoun, the Reverend Nisson (director), Arnold Welch, Earl Coffey, and Bill Davis; (second row) Fred Waswo, Carl Pickett, Ralph Marriott, Arthur Short, and Bill Collinsworth; (third row) Roy Frymire, Charles Collinsworth, Jake Ryser, Frank Eaton, Dr. Raymond, George Welch, and Harry Welch.

It is not known what band Fred Hunter is dressed up to take part in.

This band is marching in a parade in Dover. It is going from north to south on Sheridan Street with the Evangelical church, now a private residence, on the left.

September was often the time for a fair. Here is the Cashion Street Fair and Carnival for September 14–15, 1916. A band is in the distance coming up Main Street.

Even at the dawn of the 20th century, national companies sponsored floats in parades. Here is Anheuser-Busch with an early-day version of product placement. (Courtesy Kingfisher Chamber of Commerce.)

Fair day was a chance to bring one's goods to town. Here is a fair day in Hennessey about 1900.

Even small towns had baseball teams. Rivalries between towns were as intense as professional sports rivalries are today. Here is the baseball team of Kiel (later Loyal) about 1910. From left to right are (first row) Willis Spradlin and Victor Fiegel; (second row) Gus Wahling, Henry Reiswig, and Alfa Fiegel; (third row) Alvin Hoskins, Dale Murray, Charley Fiegel, and Emil Fiegel.

Here is a similar team from Hennessey. At this time, adult teams were as prominent as high school teams. It was only later that the high school teams eclipsed those of the older men.

Kingfisher had horse racing until the early 1950s. This photograph dates to the late 1940s or early 1950s. (Courtesy Carolyn Flood.)

The reason these men and women are dressed up has not been recorded, but their names have been. The picture shows Inez Rice, George Mather, June Steele, Mabel Nichols, Carl Overman, Ezra Ditterline, Ralph Miles, Lesley Lucas, Cassie Kooken, Miss Bidwell, Roxie Hockaday, Miss White, Alta Van Valkenburg, Laura Ghering, Nelle Rice, Ralph Kooken, Robert Patterson, and John Hull.

A game of cards was always a good pastime. Here are, from left to right, Abraham Jefferson Seay, Nannie Marsh, Ralph Seay, and Gertrude Sanders playing cards, probably in the Dean Hotel, which was Seay's home after his sister Isabella died in 1900 and he sold Horizon Hill. The picture is labeled "Just for Fun," but there are poker chips on the table.

Watermelon has never gone out of fashion. The first names are mostly unknown, but pictured are (first row) McCartany, Nofhiser, and Pursell; (second row) Elmer Solomon, Phillips, and Johnson.

Some rides into the country were taken just for fun.

When cars came along, riding in a new one was just the thing to do for fun. Here in about 1907 is Roxie Hockaday in the white hat in an Oldsmobile, the first big car in Kingfisher. Gordon Stone is seated next to the driver along with Ed and Sarah Hockaday, Avis Hockaday, and Lee Conn.

Sitting on the front porch could be just the thing for a lazy Sunday afternoon. This picture was taken in Kingfisher with A. H. Ruth sitting on the rail. Twila Schowalter is the small girl standing in back of the dog. A. H. Schowalter is sitting in a chair, and Mrs. Schowalter is sitting in the chair in front of the window.

Of course, there was nothing like a good glass of beer. Here Richard Pappe Sr. is pouring Gus Bollenbach some beer. Bollenbach seems to be enjoying himself.

Many still alive remember these times with great nostalgia. Here is the old courthouse, sometime before the mid-1940s, when the cupola was torn down. The old courthouse survived until 1959. Harry Brownlee is on the tricycle on the left, and Emory Brownlee is on the right, with an unidentified neighborhood boy balanced upon their shoulders.

Visit us at
arcadiapublishing.com